SIDEBROW BOOKS

SELENOGRAPHY

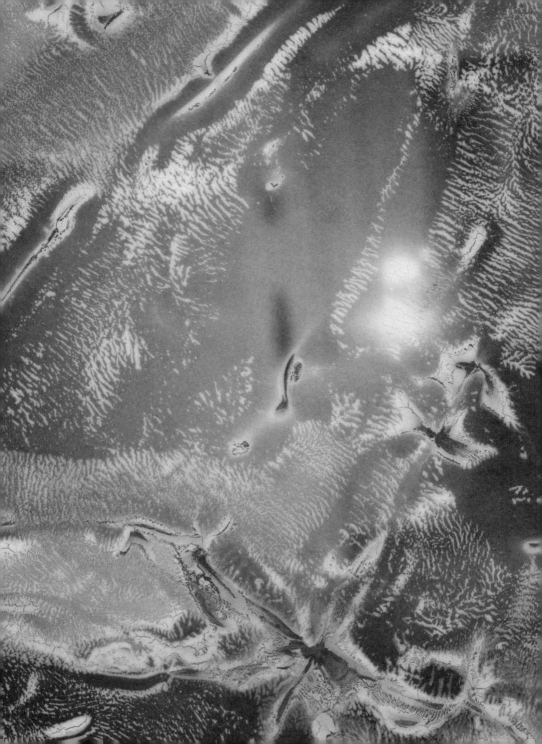

SELENOGRAPHY

JOSHUA MARIE WILKINSON

Polaroids by Tim Rutili

SIDEBROW BOOKS • 2010 • SAN FRANCISCO

Published by Sidebrow Books
912 Cole St., #162
San Francisco, CA 94117
sidebrow@sidebrow.net
www.sidebrow.net

Cover photo by Tim Rutili
Cover & book design by Jason Snyder

ISBN: 0-9814975-2-7
ISBN-13: 978-0-9814975-2-5

FIRST EDITION | FIRST PRINTING
9 8 7 6 5 4 3 2 1
SIDEBROW BOOKS 003
PRINTED IN CANADA

Sidebrow Books titles are distributed by
Small Press Distribution

Titles are available directly from Sidebrow at
www.sidebrow.net/books

A Member of
www.theintersection.org

Sidebrow is a member of the Intersection Incubator, a program of
Intersection for the Arts (www.theintersection.org) providing fiscal
sponsorship, networking, and consulting for artists. Contributions and
gifts to Sidebrow are tax-deductible to the extent allowed by law.

Excerpts of this book's texts first appeared in *The Agriculture Reader*, *Another Chicago Magazine*, *Bird Dog*, *Boston Review*, *Cannibal*, *elimae*, *Filter*, *High Chair*, *Knock*, *The Laurel Review*, *LIT*, *Redactions*, *The Seattle Review*, & *West Branch*. My thanks to the editors of these journals.

A broadside was made of an excerpt of "Wolf Dust" by Burning Chair Press (Brooklyn, 2006). Excerpts from "My Cautious Lantern" were published as the chapbook *The Book of Flashlights, Clover, & Milk* by Pilot Books (Northampton, 2008). A warm thank you to Katy and Matt Henriksen and to Betsy Wheeler as well.

Selenography is Book 1 of the *No Volta* pentalogy.

for Lily

SELENOGRAPHY

Each song
is a room
in which I'm not allowed to vanish.

— Graham Foust

MY CAUTIOUS LANTERN

the milkman's apprentice begins to heave
noise up from the road & this must

be the beginning there
are all sorts of
enemies & underlings

& mine will make liverwurst
out of us

your job is numerous more
roads but whitened with
chalk

&
I'll collect you
backwards until the rain pulls your

coat open

tumbled laundry scents accumulate
in the children's

guessing & their guessing gets sharper
some green stars

have lit up the
pond with their cold burning

one
way to mark

the spot properly is
with your eyes closed & your
lips pursed
won't you return

if horses
buckled bears
into a hem
in the woods?

snow-heavy planks &
storms enough
to

call you on
the telephone &
static your pause

I know my
photograph doesn't match
the scene it is
a good song played

too patchily
to keep
in your lungs

the moon lifts the
mucus up

my throat the windows

are also up to
no good
I could see the

saints' mouths moving through
the slot
one of

them had humongous
hands a thick
silver ring with a
jelly red

stone on
his finger we

sought
the milk of lambs in

our
neighbor's pasture we could hear crackling

we could smell horse dung &
the longest grass in the world
still my

breath got
big
while a little
can of
milk I held stayed

cold somehow

death gets curious & starts
sniffing around our
luggage

allow st. valentine
an opening & a
softer architecture

we had plums &
a handful

of soda bread
more milk a
good ball
of twine & we
tossed

the carpet onto
the skiff
& jumped on top

the river was
easy incomplete but it
took us
like twigs

polaroids
of the papier-mâché

wolves
you hear your name in

the current?

if your key finds a
lock even shakily &
if the lock
gums its advance
we will only—

into huge
snowdrifts did
the mouse
sing through the
child?
did jupiter

x
out the river?
did you return under
the right

constellation? a white cat
chewing an umbrella in the alley
somebody does

heaps of bad stuff
when the sun—*poof*
vanishes

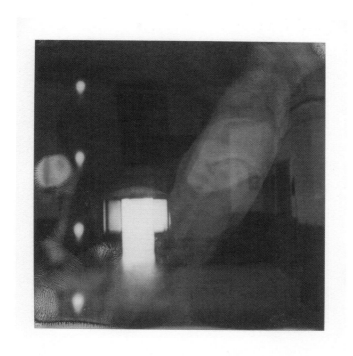

how did they
pronounce your

mother's name such that

you didn't know
who they were talking
about?

a curse has
all the ingredients
to be legendary if its

children make
room
on their forearms for drawings
of what the curse

itself might do

nobody visits the sewn-up hole
in the ceiling with flashlights

kingdom of ball-peen hammers
& rum syrup
nothing

is as unreasonable
as sunlight

stars construct
a dummy out

of your
promises you must
run twine into
the wet wall

winter will erase
parts of your hands take my

cautious
lantern & keep warm

that hatchet comes with a
boy who wields
it will the
city collapse as
a cardboard city? were
their nicknames revealed?

I say
something else I cannot
here repeat

voices get locked
in the threads & felled light
uncovers you
you drift out

WOLF DUST

the woods pulled on your
sleeve

& the bathtub water went
black your

little brother's
curtain wrapped
around your other little
brother's quiet

what light comes
between
your nightgown & you?

an owl breaks the
fold a cut tree spills

a soft crutch
hits

this dust
a freezer stocked
with I

happened
to myself in these very woods

carry your
own dancing shoes

your tin suitcase filled
with bricks & wolf dust

you are coming
through the phone wires
& ice at once

little
hunter in the chimney of

your throat

birds caught in
blocks of ice

blind colt
new bees a spun
snaky light

& laughter I know
the way
you

hold pencils to
a settling this
is the

hidden warning this
is

opened dusk
thwarting your
swallows

a fresh field
underfoot held
together between the cold radio

killer wasps
easing into the
doorjamb

a proving swamp circle of
blue flies & the reeds
chafe

toads bolster us it
is
again
nightfall

a bit
of speech scored

into the bathroom
door revolved stars dropped
us in

& we are forever here a child
spoke through

the dressmaker's dummy's cupped hand
to tell

us
again which way not
to go

a storm like
thousands of locusts
listening

not cigarettes
enough to trade us
through the

dead men
put their mouths on
the backs of

our hands little

airport slowly sank
into the
swamp with the rest
of the zoo

& its
city

a thin envelope
quicklime
goofer dust a

red telephone box
& coarse powder
for taking
the meanest layer of
skin off our backs

cuttings
shoveled

up into a fortress
hiding behind where
the dead
woman bakes lemon
& mincemeat pies
we live inside the

seam of the wind the
breaker's froth the
swarm's
sleepy landing

a pond divided

by an upside-down moon more
animals learn to hollow
grow wary

& withhold their math from us

yields memory's
search for a dancehall
with huge
aluminum ceilings
& an old water closet

a convex mirror in
the great entry
ghosts in the red
liquor

we are
reared
in the

sheepish sounds
of christmas foot-traffic
our breathing split like
a peach

we are falling sparrow-aligned
useless against

even the slenderest breeze or apologies
we are built without tools or

recording devices without the
fat whoosh of the
woodchopper

without legends
of the legendary child thieves

there was

almost nothing before us or at
our feet yet

this spinning black set negates us
names us revokes

our calls
made
in the yard the light is a foil &

it stomps
us out like a wick until our
eavesdropping is what
stuns us
awake

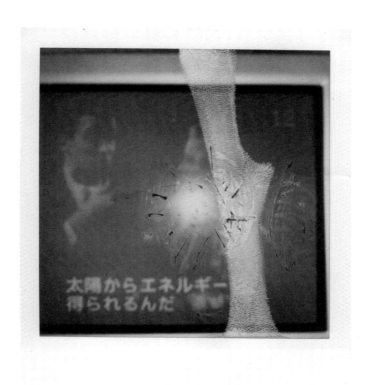

PHANTOMS IN THE TELEGRAPH INK

we row to the
center of the lake

to find the

wind's sad
shutter we move below
what now rigs the fights

thirsty we are cold &
holding just so

for what the
keyhole seems to register or
outshine in us

storybooks collecting our
ends

myths
slacken & give
out until we
hammer a new
trapdoor

powder the cracks
with
quicklime

our wrongful noise into a
city spooked
with night mortar
collating us

the stenographer's
young assistant
sets up

the apparatus
while

the silver canister waits for
not light

might finish the
waltz if their drawings

of the dancers
could be looped into
the projector

even booze
won't slow us down the
way our
construction will

what
copies out your
battles for you?
what color hands did you have

in the snow?

phantoms in
the moss phantoms
in the train cars dressed

like porters with

black eye makeup
phantoms full of
saliva &

the cottoned virus
phantoms in the telegraph

ink
grinding
their teeth now

horses follow the
messenger girl into
the wooden woods—

slowly
horses

consigned to what
no registrar can call up

we are drowsier
roused under
the coiling
wind

ready
for sirens
to quit
carving up
the city you

see somebody
is gone
&

the girl is neither
home nor
missing

the
lighthouse
is

alive
with termites &
grassy light

our sleep should collect
here from
reeling film

gone or going

A COLLATING LIGHT

a whole future marked with snow
& collating light
rabbits enough to get clean
& go
traipsing through
four cities

into a fifth an eyelash
stuck to my face
lets out a little

fleck of blood
the light blanching bilking
a strange towards —

standing around without
our arms &

voices no oath here not
even a copper
pink dusk telephone
wires spent the
lambs vanish
& gravely frost plays

landlord to the land
rotates us shaky
with speech refracted murmuring
off the
ivy wall somebody

dragging
somebody's stuff
to the street & it's been dark out for six
days which gives our music a yarn
to follow

& a little lead
in your
pencil broke
into the diary
page into
your entry
dogs appeared

a wrecked cabbage
farm nearby

gave off
a holy perfume—let's

rest
like this

kicked-in city
shorn
glass new

coal from the
vanished

things keep watch
on
other things
shoelace for a
tripwire

a man
forms his
garage

from ice

while
his mastiffs loll in

snowfall your
plastic owl wants
a word
with
me

& I give it
one

the messenger girl

nicely asks about my
sister's invisibility
there is
the moon nobody
could tie a rope to

to plane

off its edges

speed of
yellow smoke a pulled anchor through
us
your lips

are blue
in
the red light o city

why are you so
bad at
this? first

the doorway then
the story

then the bellhops
telepathy
a cordoned-off levee
as
the power
waxed

out its
own means
this movie's missing
one reel

& I
like the sounds in the projection booth
the good smell
of decayed film

& thumbtacks in the
plastery wall we
are water
& bad water mixed
together so perfectly
the township

cannot discern our
motives
from the streetscape

we are scissored out from

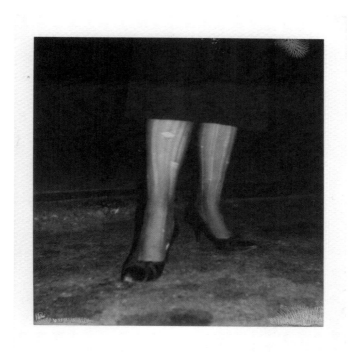

NO CLUMSY MOON TO CHALK UP
THE DOORWAY

Let me hear nothing of the moon, in my night there is no moon, and if it happens that I speak of the stars it is by mistake.

— Samuel Beckett

white letters arrived in
the city of hollowed-out
furnaces dropped through a

cut transom
&

the twins

took the letters
with the biggest swooping signatures
into the trees

to
assemble the story
of their fortress you're

soft with me
& I'm never
sorry for falling
asleep on top

of you

the radio yellowing

our adages asks
us to steady to steal without

we swim when we are
asleep no
clumsy moon
to chalk

up
the doorway where they'd

held an umbrella over the developing
tubs are listening
& writing

us down it
scores the wax in

your sister's reparation

what locksmiths us
into defenestration
& opens the hex

thirst in
private
rooms turns
off the color
& starts

lugging
parts of where you sleep

away I
follow grief in our
mighty skeletal charts says one
smeared a

room with smoke
legion in
a diarist's
electricity touches

the chopped bridge

thin sound
from the inclement front

weeping one would need
to coax
out the child
translator

from the
unlit rehearsal
when you open the waterlogged
trunk on stage

it opens your apology
with
owls rupturing
the oceanic
night another envelope drops
from our

roof as
though dust were
its own corollary as though a
translation
could rule your rules out

how to fall

down & disappear threatens
a salvo it goes

pollen pollen
parallax triptych

each

from the ghosted choristers

& a
garden of
chamomile
for the sleepless

silty river shoals turned my
brother down like a bed

strange glow
so out

trains christen a
thimble
the jaw & our message
from the meadow
finds out this secret so your

job is to hide in
how the
dark
is thick enough
to

out here in the icy throes
of what winter dilutes
in our custodial
hearts
says

invisible like it's
a verb
from the shed of
stolen objects

lacuna
means the
beginning owns you

not that the iron
door needs you

but that what you need
belongs to what

the door is
made to keep out summoning

a new history of light
up from the earth

in the signature
swallows
unseam the silvery ocean
for I am holding
this
canticle

to
the hollow of my throat

wooden song
in my
sleeve or alone

faintest blood

in your tall beer
the elevator's milky
odor gives you your

darkroom voice

until you're asleep
standing holding your own hands
together like bricks

dandelion milk in
a vial

moths from the library basement
we're never to go
in search of

cellar door
in your
approximations

loosened the huge rabbits
from the blanket dipped in

salt in red
tea

hello bottom
of
the lake a

subtle inquiry without
words go

slightly down

go slightly down
with the atlassed ones

a whispering rends
the antidote into
code

no memory can pull down the wind
but one

watching for bees to
foil distance between us
& the light of our projected
photographs

makes a bid
darns us

no togethering to
wall up or shine us forth

a widow works the net

the phonebooth charters
the moon

what armors the birds?

turned the dancers
to vellum

the street into crocus
buds with a shiver

turned the motel
towels into a breeze

because casting
spells loosens us off

no little cats to
creep past no

stars to withdraw from
the child's palm

I draw you a bath & a picture a little
letter forth

there is no love without
strangers in the street
with their murmuring
like wires

a knock at the
wall

a chalk line to cross says the boy
with the trapdoor in his eye

I have a fold I
have no followable paths

Joshua Marie Wilkinson is the author of four other books of poetry.
He lives in Chicago and Athens, Georgia.

Tim Rutili plays in the band Califone. He lives in Los Angeles and Chicago.

SIDEBROW BOOKS | www.sidebrow.net

SIDEBROW 01 ANTHOLOGY

A multi-threaded, collaborative narrative, featuring work by
65 writers of innovative poetry and prose

SB001 | ISBN: 0-9814975-0-0 | DECEMBER 2008

ON WONDERLAND & WASTE

Sandy Florian

Collages by Alexis Anne Mackenzie

SB002 | ISBN: 0-9814975-1-9 | APRIL 2010

SELENOGRAPHY

Joshua Marie Wilkinson

Polaroids by Tim Rutili

SB003 | ISBN: 0-9814975-2-7 | APRIL 2010

To order, and to view information on new and forthcoming titles,
visit www.sidebrow.net/books.